A GIFT FOR

FROM

With love to Steve Jackson,
my husband, best friend,
and partner in pill caddies.
—M.W.

Published by Hallmark Gift Books,
a division of Hallmark Cards, Inc.,
Kansas City, MO 64141
Visit us on the Web at Hallmark.com.

Editorial Director: Delia Berrigan
Editor: Kim Schworm Acosta
Art Director: Chris Opheim
Designer and Illustrator: Mary Eakin
Production Designer: Dan Horton
Lead Writer: Molly Wigand
Contributing Writers: Chris Conti, Allyson Cook,
Matt Gowen, Bill Gray, Tina Neidlein, Dan Taylor

ISBN: 978-1-63059-005-5
BOK2277

Made in China
1016

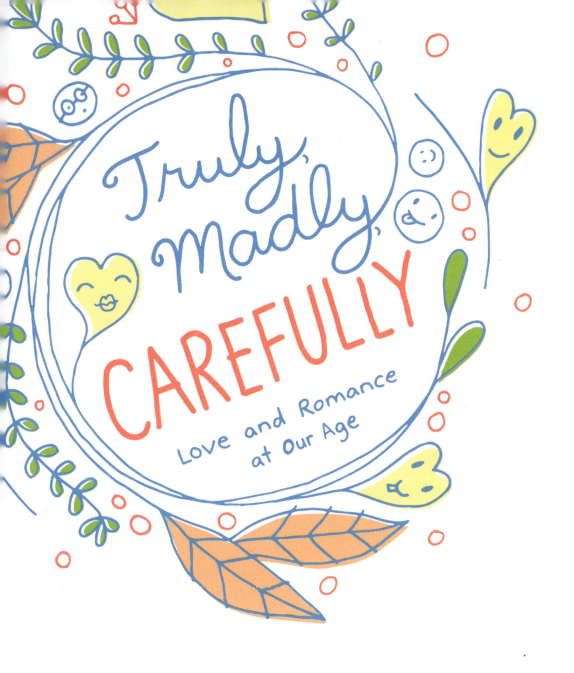

Truly, Madly, CAREFULLY

Love and Romance at Our Age

By Molly Wigand and Friends

Hallmark

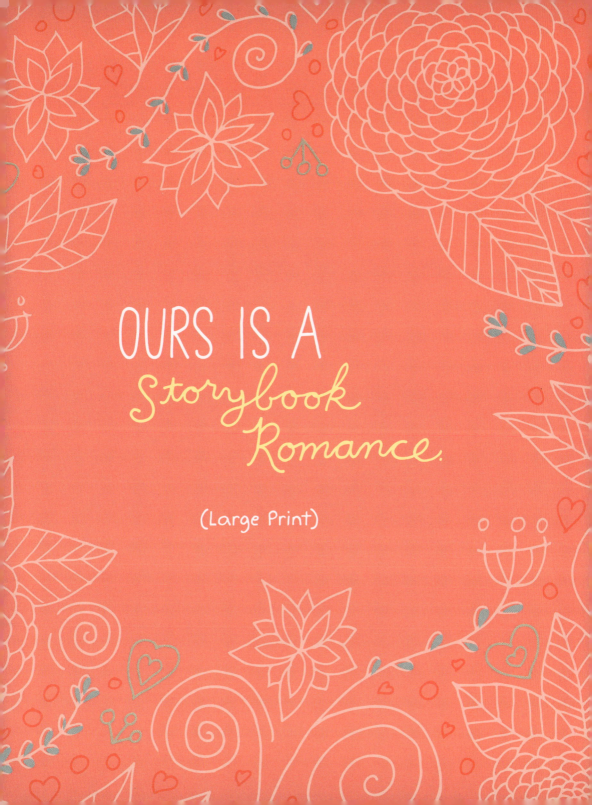

OURS IS A
Storybook
Romance.

(Large Print)

We're at a place where
we both understand that

HOT, YOUNG LOVE

is vastly overrated and
would conflict with our shows.

I love our credo:

DANCE

like no one's standing by
with an ice pack.

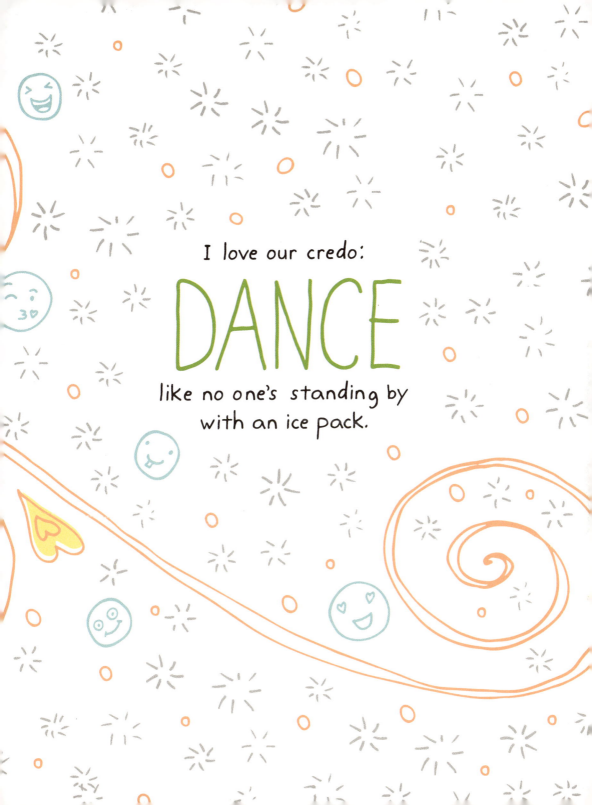

YOU'RE THE
BEE'S KNEES.

(A young bee. Not a bee our age.)

Is it footsie or just
a shameless attempt to
warm up our icy-cold feet?

Love that we agree
on the important
things in life.

Like whose turn it is to
wash the dishes.

(NOT MINE!)

We have the best threesomes...

you, me, and the DVR.

There's nothing more romantic for a couple our age than overcooking dinner together.

You are

THE GIN

to my Metamucil®.

It's a miracle we found each other.

We can never find

ANYTHING.

I wanna hold your hand.

Especially when I'm
trying to figure out
something on the computer.

SO SCARY!

If we have to jump into the

FLAVORLESS PIT

of a no-salt, grease-free lifestyle,
at least we have each other.

TOGETHER WE WORK.

You (and/or a flight of stairs)
take my breath away.

Also, watch out, because you might
go near it if you don't hear it.

We could sign up for classes
at the community college
but let's not.

YOUNG, FIRM, AND IN LOVE!

Well, one out of three
ain't bad.

All we need is love,
unless we're out of decaf.

I love that brushing our teeth
together counts as foreplay and
sleeping counts as sex.

Let's not ever get laser eye surgery
and mess up our

BLISSFULLY BLURRY
LOVEMAKING.

Two is always better than one.

Unless we're talking knee replacements.

What happens at Grandma's
makes Grandma very tired.

GOT THAT, GRANDPA?

Together, there's nothing we can't do.

Except crowds, loud restaurants,
and just about anything past 9 p.m.

OUR LOVE ENDURES.

Like those random hairs.

Learning new things together is fun.

The same goes for flinging new
technology at the wall.

I guess we could share our

LOVE SECRETS

with the media.

But at our age, who needs
one more leak?

OUR LOVE
GROWS BIGGER.

Yet we get shorter.

Science is funny like that.

I always wanted us to grow old together.
So we can check *that* off the list.

17 ☐ =
18 ☐ = 36 ☐ = 54 ☐ =
19 ☐ = 37 ☐ = 55 ☐ =
20 ☐ = 38 ☐ = 56 ☐
21 ☐ = 39 ☐ = 57 ☐
22 ☐ = 40 ☐ = 58 ☐ =
23 ☐ = 41 ☐ = 59 ☐
24 ☐ = 42 ☑ ♡ 60 ☐
25 ☐ = 43 ☐ = 61 ☐ =
26 ☐ = 44 ☐ = 62 ☐ =
27 ☐ = 45 ☐ = 63 ☐ =
28 ☐ = 46 ☐ = 64 ☐ =
29 ☐ = 47 ☐ = 65 ☐ =
30 ☐ = 48 ☐ = 66 ☐ =
31 ☐ = 49 ☐ = 67 ☐ =

I love you

24/7.

About the same
amount of time we
watch the news.

Our current words to live by:
Spicy foods, bad. Spicy love,

GOOD.

Love means never having to

take a taxi to our colonoscopies.

Let's have a romantic dinner
at the best restaurant in town . . .

you know, the one with the
comfy chairs and no loud music.

I love that
we never hold grudges
against each other.

We simply don't have the
memory capacity.

I LOVE OUR ADVENTURES!

Like sneaking snacks from
home into the movies.

We could do worse than each other.

And have.

One advantage of love at
our age is knowing when to
just shut up.

We go together like TV movies and falling asleep during TV movies.

Our love is like a
roller coaster. Full of

THRILLS, CHILLS,

and possible heart risks.

We don't have to rock 'n' roll all night.

An hour or two of oldies music before
bedtime sounds like plenty to me.

Love is when we save each other
the last antacid tablet.

We still find it exciting to
"GET A ROOM."

Movies on Demand,
minibar,
Posturepedic® mattress...
What's not to like?

No décor is more homey than
our matching butt dents
in the sofa.

"YES!
RIGHT THERE!
MORE! MORE!"

I love our late-night foot rubs.

Our parents need us.
Our kids need us.
But let us never forget that
our local bars need us, too.

Our love just keeps
getting stronger.

Must be all those
calcium supplements.

The first rule of senior sex is

DON'T

call it senior sex.

In a healthy relationship,
each partner has hobbies—
like sports, reading, and complaining
about the other person's hobbies.

Travel for us is doing the same
things in a different place.

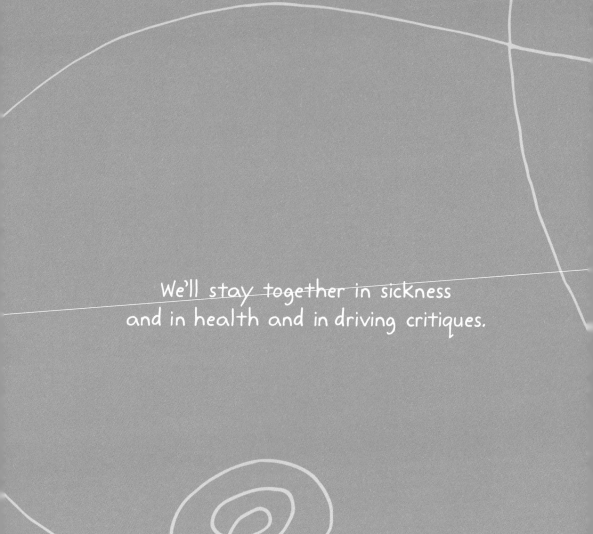

We'll stay together in sickness
and in health and in driving critiques.

A romance like ours will

NEVER COOL OFF.

Mostly because of how high
we keep the thermostat.

Love will keep us together.

Also debt.

With you by my side,
I have everything I need.

But if you get up, can you make me a sandwich?

HEAD OVER HEELS

tonight means a painful trip
to urgent care tomorrow.

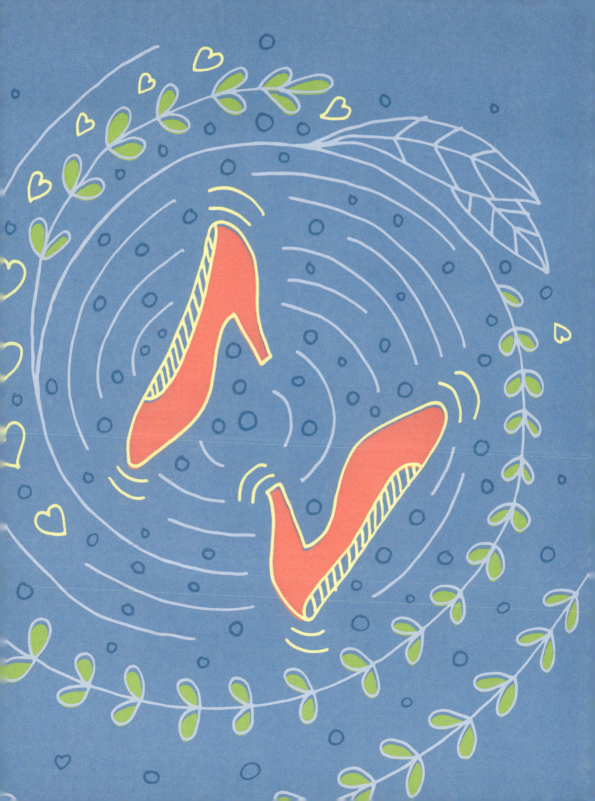

Together, we can face anything.
Mostly, the TV. We face the TV a lot.

Stronger than brand-new bifocals,
thicker than oatmeal,
hotter than a fresh pot of decaf...

THAT'S US.

Our love is sweeter
than all the foods we're
not supposed to be
eating anymore.

I love that we can still enjoy
our favorite sexual position...

AWAKE.

Our love proves that the
best things in life are free. . . .
or at the very least come
with a senior discount.

-2%

We can weather

ANY STORM.

Mostly because we'll refuse
to go out in it.

At our age, it's best if we
don't lie in bed for too long.

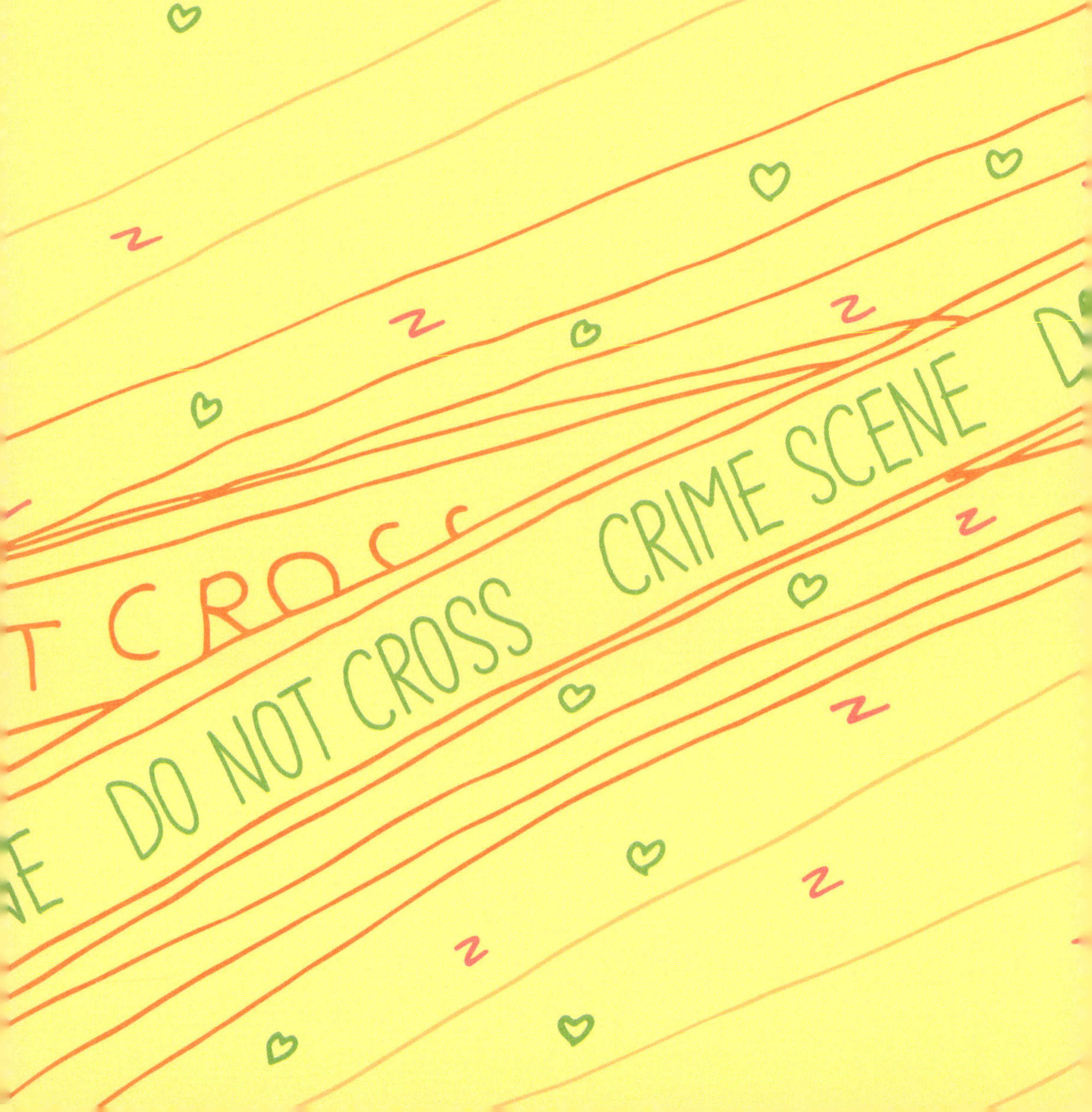

CRIME SCENE

T CRO

DO NOT CROSS

Someone might suspect
foul play.

The best part about travel is
helping each other get the feeling
back in the numb parts.

We've got our love plus about a
dozen comforters to keep us warm.

OUR LOVE IS BLIND.

Drugstore glasses help, though.

Nothing can stop our love,
although sudden leg cramps
may slow it down.

I'd "slip into something more comfortable," but most of the time, I'm already in sweatpants.

You make my heart

SKIP A BEAT.

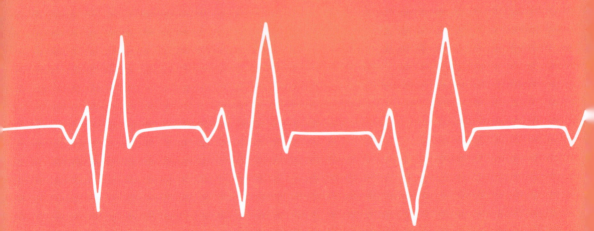

**If you have enjoyed this book
or it has touched your life in some way,
we would love to hear from you.**

Please send your comments to:
Hallmark Book Feedback
P.O. Box 419034
Mail Drop 100
Kansas City, MO 64141

Or e-mail us at:
booknotes@hallmark.com

At least I hope it's you.